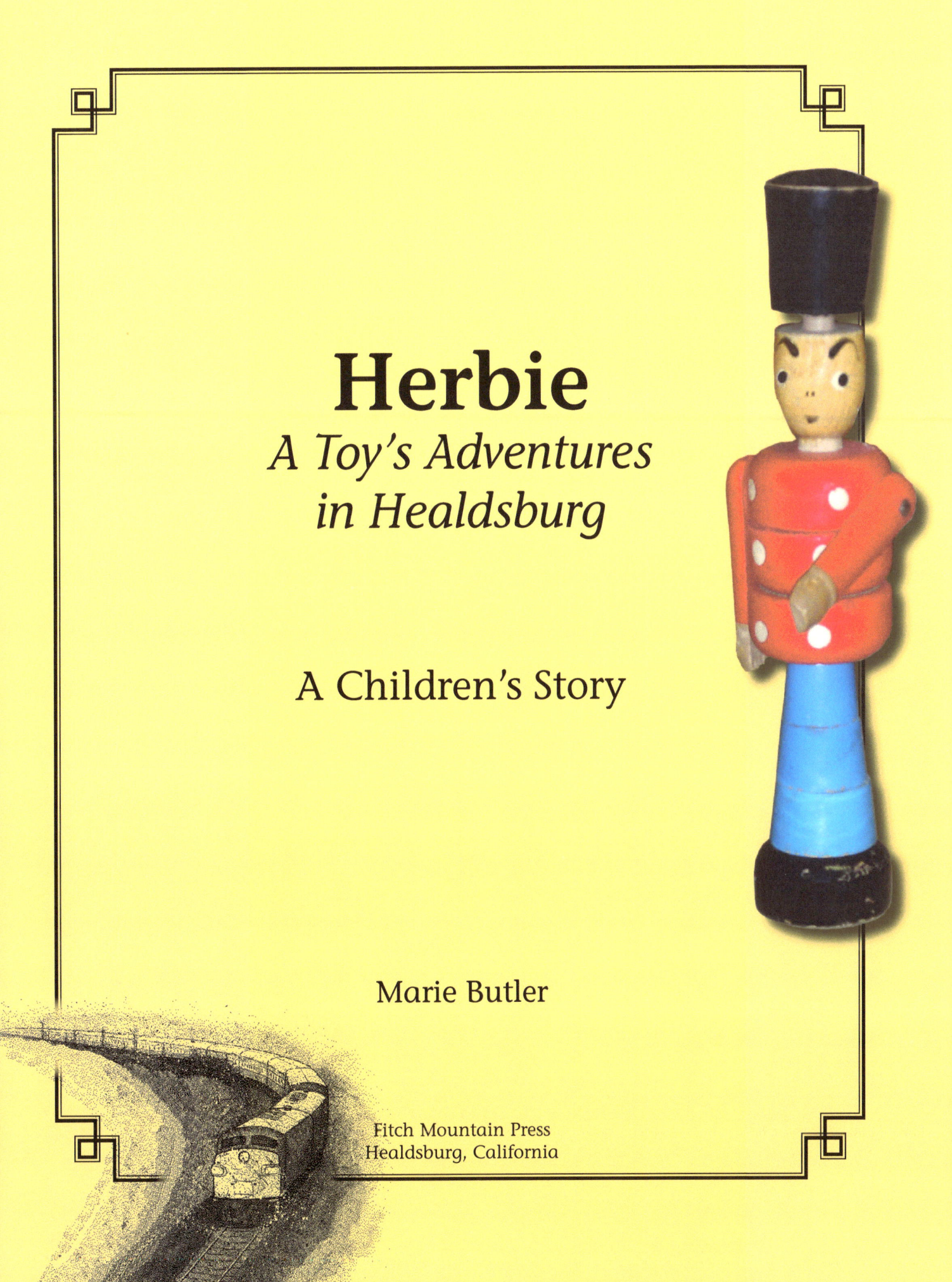

To Corey, who was born with an adventurer's spirit.

Acknowledgements

Deep gratitude goes to Holly Hoods of the Healdsburg Museum; she is patient, knowledgeable and has a true love of Healdsburg. Thanks, too, to Al Loebel for photoshopping Herbie into Healdsburg's history. I appreciate the support and advice of my writing pals in "the group"—Preble Franklin, Dick Perce and Bill Hanson. Camille Picott and Ted Calvert were very generous in sharing their information and experiences. Thanks to Pete Masterson for his help—he knows all about the publishing world. Finally, thank you to all my family and friends for their assistance during this project. It was an "adventure!"

Copyright © 2011 by Marie Butler. All Rights Reserved. No part of this book may be reproduced, electronically stored, or transmitted in any form by any means, electronic, mechanical, photocopied, recorded, or otherwise, without the prior written permission of the publisher.

ISBN: 978-0-9831463-0-8

Published by
Fitch Mountain Press
Healdsburg, California

Historic photos courtesy of Healdsburg Museum and Historical Society.

Printed in the United States of America

In the Beginning

"The first thing I remember is when the toymaker painted on my eyes," the little toy soldier recounted. He turned to his companion on the Museum's closet shelf, a small brass dog with droopy ears who had been the Fire Department's mascot since 1939.

"Go on," said Dog.

"First he did my left eye, then my right. I blinked — I could see! I moved my jointed arms a little; squeak went one. The old toymaker frowned at the sound and took out a little copper oilcan with a spout. 'Splurt,' went the oil, right into my joint. Ahh, that was better."

"Well, Hobie," said the old man. *"Ja,* now you are done! Be a good toy and have a good life."

And he put me on a shelf to dry. *"Hobie,"* I thought. *"So that's my name."*

When the toymaker left for the night, I glanced around the shop. In the dim light I saw yellow ducks on wheels, perky marionettes, ballerinas poised on their toes and a green train with red wheels; all of us carved from wood. I looked down at my bright red and blue uniform with white buttons. *"Well, I AM a handsome lad,"* I thought. *"I will be an excellent toy!"*

The year was 1955, according to the radio in the shop, and my fellow toys and I were living in Denmark. One day, an American soldier walked into the toy store. When I heard the jingling bell above the door, I just knew that this was the day… this was when I could begin my life as a good toy!

The soldier wore a fine uniform, though I thought mine was shinier. He glanced around the shop and spotted me. I stood taller, ready to salute, if necessary.

"Hey," he said, "you'd be a swell gift for my kid brother, Mark!" So I was wrapped in crisp tissue and tucked into a neat brown paper bag. "OK, pal, you're going on an adventure," the soldier told me. First, we flew to his base in Germany. The plane hummed and bumped. After a few days, we left and took another, long airplane trip: "home," to Healdsburg, California, USA.

I took a breath and turned to Dog, who had been listening patiently.

"Well," he yawned, "that was a long time ago. What have you been doing since then? How did you end up here?"

Dog was a good audience. Better, I thought, than the fuzzy, grey cat one shelf down on the right. The Museum people had gone home; we had all night. So, I began the Healdsburg portion of my tale.

Arriving Home in Healdsburg

When David (for that was the soldier's name) arrived home, he had gifts for everyone; his parents, two sisters and brother.

"Wow, he's keen!" said Mark when David pulled me out of his rucksack, un-crinkling the tissue paper. I glanced around at all these smiling people… and at King, the big, brown and white family dog. King looked up hopefully. His bushy tail thumped on the linoleum floor.

"No, King, he's my toy," Mark said to the dog. King snuffled.

Mark ran next door to show me to his best friend, Ken, with King trotting closely behind; Mark and his pal lived in Victorian houses on Matheson Street. Ken and his sister were sitting in their living room, watching cartoons on the Zenith black and white television.

"What's his name?" his sister asked when she saw me.

"Name?" thought Mark, turning me over. "Name?" he said aloud.

"Just ask him!" she demanded.

I stared into Mark's eyes and concentrated hard. *"Hobie,"* I tried silently to tell Mark.

"Herbie!" Mark cried.

"Close enough," I thought.

It was late summer. A light dust from the nearby orchards settled on the steps and sidewalks of town; the heavy smell of sweet, drying prunes filled the air.

Our afternoons were spent on the Russian River. Mark and Ken counted tadpoles and made mud forts; I was the guard. Or, they'd sit me in a little wooden boat and pull me along against the current, pretending I was in the town's water ski race near Memorial Bridge. "Go, Herbie," they'd cheer. King would dive into the green-blue water, splash us, and then run happily down the beach, coming back muddy and wet.

Sometimes, Mark and Ken would take me with them for a cool soda at The Office Fountain near the Plaza. I'd stand at attention next to the tall glasses overflowing with ice cream and chocolate syrup. We'd get sticky when cold, little rivers of cream spilled over and slipped onto the counter.

"That's how I got my first scratch." I said to Dog. "See the nick right here on my hat? I rolled right off the counter onto the floor."

"Hardly shows," said Dog. "Now, I could tell you stories from the old Fire House…"

"Yes," I interrupted him, "...my first scratch. But, it was King, who accidently caused most of my scrapes. He thought I was his toy, too. It started at the downtown Plaza." I continued...

After eating fried chicken at the Ice Berg restaurant down West Street, the family met friends for a Saturday evening band concert. Conductor Owen Sweeten was doing a grand job. Mark waved me like the conductor's baton, keeping the beat to a rousing John Philip Sousa march.

We sat near the water fountain. Mark's baby sister, Meg, was holding King's brown leather leash, while he slept at her feet. Suddenly, the cymbals crashed and King jumped up. The noise surprised Mark and he dropped me. In a second as thin as a dog's whisker, King snatched me up and ran to the fountain. Plop! Splash! He plunked me into the basin, then ran back to Meg, laughing a doggie laugh and very proud of himself.

Mark's dad reached in and fished me out.

"King was saving you?" Dog asked. I nodded. I thought so, then.

Time Passed

Fall and school days came quickly. Winters were wet and the River flooded its banks. Mark, Meg and I stayed inside playing with Lincoln Logs; sometimes I was the general, sometimes a pioneer. On those cold days, King would stretch out by the fireplace with its snapping flames; Meg would dress him in a big, knitted doll sweater. On rainy Saturdays, we went to the Aven Theatre.

Soon it was late spring; the prune trees were in blossom and another summer was in the air. It was the last day of school. Meg and I were sitting on the porch steps. She had dressed me in her doll's hula skirt, in honor of Hawaii becoming the 50th state. She called me her Hula Herbie.

King had been visiting with his doggie pal, Champ, a tan dachshund three doors down, and was now dozing on the top step, waiting for Mark to come home from school.

"That dog sleeps all day," said Mama from the screen door. She had been canning strawberry jam and wiped her hands on her apron. "You'd think King was up all night!"

King rolled over at the sound of his name, took one look at me in a hula skirt and howled: *"ah-ooooh!"* He scrambled to his feet, grabbed me on the run and dashed to the sidewalk.

"Trying to save you again," said Dog, wisely.

"Yup," I replied. "But, when King dropped me on the concrete, I split clean in half! Parts of me were everywhere. I lost my white belt." I shook my head sadly, from side to side. "I had never been out of uniform before."

"How did you get put back together?" Dog asked.

"Meg's older sister, Julie, helped. She found spare parts in their dad's shop behind the house. But, she was in a hurry. And, well… I'm embarrassed to say, I'm mixed up."

Dog squinted. "Where?"

"Don't you see? My red and blue uniform parts are piled on upside down. I look lumpy this way! And, I rattle without my belt.

"Well, you look OK to me," Dog replied, distracted by a fire truck's horn in the distance. "Oh, that sounds like Engine No. 6381, heading down Johnson Street."

I waved my arm. "Not OK," I told him. "That was also the summer of the River Bandit."

The River Bandit Strikes Again

The Bandit — yes, that summer things went missing from Matheson and Fitch Street porches and yards. Strange objects were taken: a ragdoll, a scarf, six cookies Mrs. Smith had just bought from Fred's French Bakery and even Champ's favorite dog bone. The only evidence left behind was an occasional clump of River mud on the porches or backstairs. The neighbors were stumped. Who would want old toys and odds and ends?

My family had just come in from an evening at Palomar Roller Rink where Meg dropped me only once as we twirled around the rink. Mark's mama and Aunt Alice sat in wicker chairs on the broad front porch, discussing the Bandit. Even though it was 8:30 at night, the day's heat lingered. Meg was pretending the porch railing was a castle and that I was a knight. King was behind a potted plant, snoring, his muddy paws in the air. Mama fanned herself with a dishtowel embroidered with a red rooster. She had tuned in the living room radio to KSRO; *"Hot diggity dog ziggity boom…"* came sifting through the screens and open windows.

"I'm just not used to this weather," declared Aunt Alice, who was visiting from San Francisco. She removed her purple beaded necklace and placed it on the small wicker table nearby. "Guess I'm tired from the trip. I'm going to turn in now."

"Good idea," agreed Mama. And so, scooting a tired Meg upstairs, they went to bed.

"Hey, wait," I called out. *"What about me?"* I had been left outside, with King.

Later that night, the Bandit quietly carried his loot down the street. Only the crickets, an old owl and Mrs. Pringle's cat, Midnight, saw him head toward West Street… and they weren't talking.

He walked swiftly past the Old Cemetery and Plaza, past Carroll's Pharmacy and the dusty Nock's Feed Store with one goal in mind: to hide his latest treasures. He went to his usual spot, a weedy area near the railroad tracks next to the old hobo encampment, and dug a hole. He hid his goodies near the blue Maxwell House coffee cans left behind by the hobos when they hopped on freight trains running to the north.

First into the hole went Aunt Alice's necklace, followed by the rooster dishtowel and other treats. He made a second trip up Matheson Street to bring back Herbie, his special treasure.

"Wait, where are we going? It's dark!" Herbie called, sleepily.

Thud! The Bandit dropped Herbie on top of the towel. As the Bandit turned to leave, there was a soft "clunk" as something else accidently fell into the hole; a silver dog tag.

"Ah well," Herbie thought. "Mark and Meg will find me." He settled into the dishtowel. Far out on Westside Road, a car horn honked twice. Much later, he felt the rumble of a train clanking by. A gopher nudged the towel once, looking for roots.

"Any minute, now… they'll find me." Herbie yawned. And, then he fell asleep.

The next morning, when Meg went outside to get Herbie, he was gone! As Mama and Aunt Alice searched, they discovered the necklace and dishtowel were missing, too.

They looked everywhere; Mark and David helped search. Nothing.

"Herbie!" Meg wailed. And, finally, they could only conclude that the River Bandit had struck again.

And so, it became family lore. Mark and his brother and sisters would get together on hot summer nights and tell the tale about "the summer Herbie was stolen by the River Bandit." They told it first to their children and as years went on, to grandchildren. The story always ended the same: *"...the Bandit was never caught — and, Herbie was never found."*

While Herbie was sleeping...

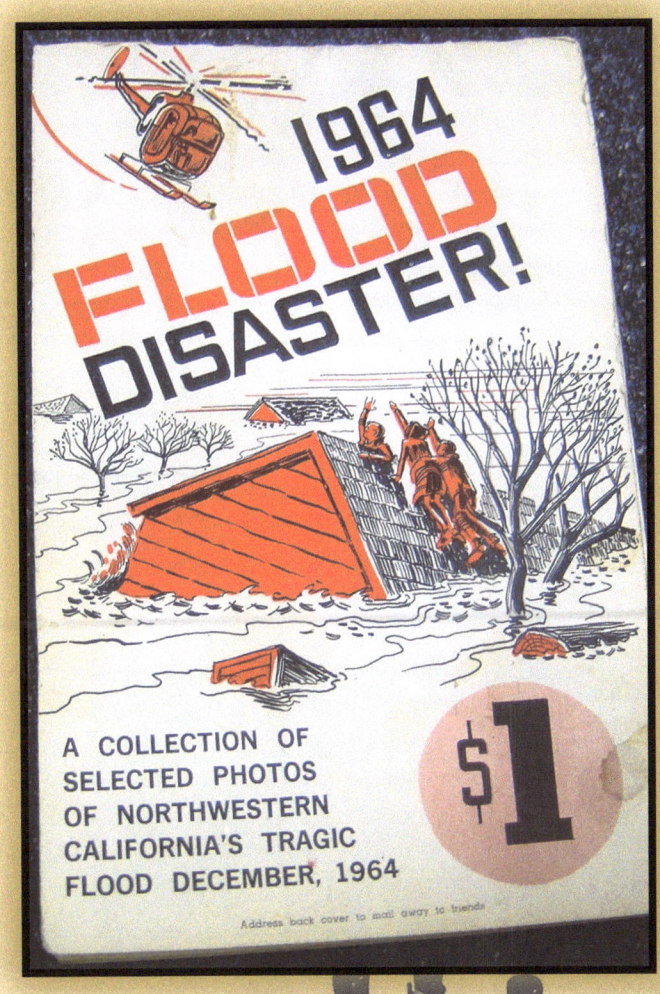

I Wake Up

Almost twenty years passed since the summer of the River Bandit. A work crew was excavating near the railroad tracks, repairing the road near the new shopping center.

"Hey Smitty," one worker called to his crew chief. "Look what I found!"

Smitty leaned over and brushed leaves, straw and dirt aside. There were half a dozen rusted coffee cans. "Humph, leftovers from the hobos, I guess," he said, turning away.

"There's stuff mixed up here, boss," the worker persisted.

Smitty moved aside one can and saw scraps of fabric, a dusty purple necklace… and me!

"Hey, would you look at this!" Smitty said, gathering up the contents.

"And what are you doing here, little hobo?" he said, blowing the grit off my face.

"Not hobo… Herbie!" I croaked out, but he didn't hear me.

The necklace was tangled in the shredded cloth. As Smitty pulled at it, a tarnished, silver dog tag dropped out. He picked it up and tried to make out the tag's imprint: "King," it read, with a phone number. "Idlewood 3…" was all he could read.

Smitty gathered up the odd collection and carried it to the nearby Police Department at City Hall.

As he set me onto the counter, I glanced out the window and saw the redwood trees in the Plaza. They were much taller than I remembered.

"You might be interested in these," Smitty said to the officers, relating where he found the amusing treasure trove. "And, take good care of little hobo, here."

"Herbie!" I said again.

"They stored me in the old Carnegie Library, until the new Museum was ready. And, that's how I ended up here," I explained to Dog.

"Well, welcome to our group," said Dog. "Just ignore the furry cat on the lower shelf. He snores. Say…" he added, "who WAS the Bandit?"

"Can't you guess?" I answered. "It was big, muddy-pawed King."

A Reunion

The holiday displays were ready. The winter sun twinkled through the glass front door. Evergreen scents filled the top floor of the Museum, and visitors strolled past cases with fuzzy teddy bears and bright-eyed dolls. On one wall were tiny Pomo Indian baskets. Quilts made of colorful squares and arrowheads from the 1800s drew an interested crowd as did a little train going round and round.

Herbie stood next to his pal, Dog; they were part of the Museum's toy exhibit.

A woman walked by with her little granddaughter. She glanced at Herbie, and then stopped abruptly.

"Granny!" the little girl cried in surprise, bumping into her grandmother.

"Mark," the woman called out to her older brother across the room. "Mark, come here."

"Meg, shhhh," said the grey-haired man as he walked over. "What…" He saw where she was pointing.

"It's Herbie!" they both said at the same time.

"Herbie — hey, how are you, old buddy?" Mark grinned.

"How did he get here?" Meg asked, bewildered.

"Can I help you?" Holly, the Museum Curator overheard them. "Did you have some questions about our boy here?"

Did they! When and how did Herbie land there, they wanted to know. Where had he been?

Holly tried to explain. But, in the years since he was discovered at the hobo camp, details about Herbie were forgotten. No record was found, she said. He had just appeared on a back shelf in the Museum years ago.

"Really? Well, we can tell you about Herbie!" And, Mark and Meg shared their funny memories of Herbie. They told her how he went missing that hot summer night and about the River Bandit.

"We had a big dog back then who just loved Herbie, too," they told Holly.

"Well, since you're his real owners, maybe he should go home with you…" Holly started to say.

Mark and Meg looked at each other, in silent agreement. "No," Mark told Holly, "Herbie earned his retirement. He was a ***great*** toy. Let other children enjoy him here."

Herbie was content, too.

"I just knew they'd find me," he said, glancing down at Dog.

Mark and Meg brought their families to visit him at least once a year. And, since Herbie still had adventure stories to tell other toys as they arrived, he was happy.

"Besides," he told Dog, "what would you do without me? Now, tell me again about the mysterious fire on Fitch Mountain that burned old Frenchy's cabin."

"Well, it was a hot summer night, 50 years ago…," Dog began.

www.ingramcontent.com/pod-product-compliance
Lightning Source LLC
Chambersburg PA
CBHW042019090426
42811CB00015B/1687